Playlist Title

Dedicated to

Date

Song Name	Artist	Year	Notes

URL

Notes

Playlist Title

Dedicated to   Date

Song Name	Artist	Year	Notes

URL

Notes

Playlist Title

Dedicated to

Date

Song Name	Artist	Year	Notes

URL

Notes

Playlist Title

Dedicated to   Date

Song Name	Artist	Year	Notes

URL

Notes

Playlist Title

Dedicated to ___________________________   Date ___________

Song Name	Artist	Year	Notes

URL ___________________________

Notes ___________________________

Playlist Title

Dedicated to _______________________________   Date _________

Song Name	Artist	Year	Notes

URL ____

Notes ____

Playlist Title

Dedicated to ________________________ Date ________

Song Name	Artist	Year	Notes

URL ________________________

Notes ________________________

Playlist Title

Dedicated to ______________________________   Date ________

Song Name	Artist	Year	Notes

URL ____

Notes ____

Playlist Title

Dedicated to ___________________________ Date ___________

Song Name	Artist	Year	Notes

URL ___________________________

Notes ___________________________

Playlist Title

Dedicated to ______________________ Date ______

Song Name	Artist	Year	Notes

URL ______________________

Notes ______________________

Playlist Title

Dedicated to _______________________   Date _______

Song Name	Artist	Year	Notes

URL _______________________________________

Notes _______________________________________

Playlist Title

Dedicated to   Date

Song Name	Artist	Year	Notes

URL

Notes

Playlist Title

Dedicated to   Date

Song Name	Artist	Year	Notes

URL

Notes

Playlist Title

Dedicated to   Date

Song Name	Artist	Year	Notes

URL

Notes

Playlist Title

Dedicated to ___________________________ Date __________

Song Name	Artist	Year	Notes

URL ___________________________

Notes ___________________________

Playlist Title _______________________________

Dedicated to _____________________ Date _______

Song Name	Artist	Year	Notes

URL _______________________________

Notes _______________________________

Playlist Title ________________________________

Dedicated to ___________________________   Date __________

Song Name	Artist	Year	Notes

URL ____

Notes ____

Playlist Title

Dedicated to   Date

Song Name	Artist	Year	Notes

URL

Notes

Playlist Title

Dedicated to ____________________________   Date ________

Song Name	Artist	Year	Notes

URL ____

Notes ____

Playlist Title

Dedicated to __________ Date __________

Song Name	Artist	Year	Notes

URL __________

Notes __________

Playlist Title

Dedicated to   Date

Song Name	Artist	Year	Notes

URL

Notes

Playlist Title

Dedicated to   Date

Song Name	Artist	Year	Notes

URL

Notes

Playlist Title

Dedicated to   Date

Song Name	Artist	Year	Notes

URL

Notes

Playlist Title

Dedicated to   Date

Song Name	Artist	Year	Notes

URL

Notes

Playlist Title

Dedicated to __________________________   Date ________

Song Name	Artist	Year	Notes

URL __________________________

Notes __________________________

Playlist Title

Dedicated to ___________________________________ Date ___________

Song Name	Artist	Year	Notes

URL ___________________________________

Notes ___________________________________

Playlist Title _______________

Dedicated to _______________   Date _______________

Song Name	Artist	Year	Notes

URL _______________

Notes _______________

Playlist Title

Dedicated to ____________________________ Date ________

Song Name	Artist	Year	Notes

URL ____

Notes ______________________________________

Playlist Title

Dedicated to

Date

Song Name	Artist	Year	Notes

URL

Notes

Playlist Title

Dedicated to   Date

Song Name	Artist	Year	Notes

URL

Notes

Playlist Title

Dedicated to _______________________________   Date _______

Song Name	Artist	Year	Notes

URL _______________________________

Notes _______________________________

Playlist Title

Dedicated to

Date

Song Name	Artist	Year	Notes

URL

Notes

Playlist Title

Dedicated to   Date

Song Name	Artist	Year	Notes

URL

Notes

Playlist Title

Dedicated to ________________________________ Date ________

Song Name	Artist	Year	Notes

URL ____

Notes ____

Playlist Title

Dedicated to ___________________________   Date _______

Song Name	Artist	Year	Notes

URL ___________________________

Notes ___________________________

Playlist Title

Dedicated to   Date

Song Name	Artist	Year	Notes

URL

Notes

Playlist Title

Dedicated to ___________________________   Date ___________

Song Name	Artist	Year	Notes

URL ____

Notes ____

Playlist Title

Dedicated to ___________________________   Date _______

Song Name	Artist	Year	Notes

URL ____

Notes ____

Playlist Title

Dedicated to ___________________________   Date ________

Song Name	Artist	Year	Notes

URL ____

Notes ____

Playlist Title

Dedicated to   Date

Song Name	Artist	Year	Notes

URL

Notes

Playlist Title

Dedicated to   Date

Song Name	Artist	Year	Notes

URL

Notes

Playlist Title

Dedicated to   Date

Song Name	Artist	Year	Notes

URL

Notes

Playlist Title

Dedicated to ___________________________   Date _______

Song Name	Artist	Year	Notes

URL ___________________________

Notes ___________________________

Playlist Title

Dedicated to _______________________ Date _______

Song Name	Artist	Year	Notes

URL _______________________

Notes _______________________

Playlist Title

Dedicated to   Date

Song Name	Artist	Year	Notes

URL

Notes

Playlist Title

Dedicated to _______________________ Date ________

Song Name	Artist	Year	Notes

URL ________________________________

Notes ______________________________

Playlist Title

Dedicated to ___________________________ Date ___________

Song Name	Artist	Year	Notes

URL ___________________________

Notes ___________________________

Playlist Title

Dedicated to _______________________ Date _______

Song Name	Artist	Year	Notes

URL _______________________

Notes _______________________

Playlist Title

Dedicated to   Date

Song Name	Artist	Year	Notes

URL

Notes

Playlist Title

Dedicated to ______________________________ Date ________

Song Name	Artist	Year	Notes

URL ______________________________

Notes ______________________________

Playlist Title

Dedicated to   Date

Song Name	Artist	Year	Notes

URL

Notes

Playlist Title

Dedicated to   Date

Song Name	Artist	Year	Notes

URL

Notes

Playlist Title

Dedicated to ___________________________   Date __________

Song Name	Artist	Year	Notes

URL ___________________________

Notes ___________________________

Playlist Title

Dedicated to ___________________________   Date _______

Song Name	Artist	Year	Notes

URL ___________________________

Notes ___________________________

Playlist Title

Dedicated to   Date

Song Name	Artist	Year	Notes

URL

Notes

Playlist Title

Dedicated to ___________________________   Date ___________

Song Name	Artist	Year	Notes

URL ___________________________

Notes ___________________________

Playlist Title

Dedicated to ______________________ Date __________

Song Name	Artist	Year	Notes

URL ______________________________

Notes ______________________________

Playlist Title ___________________________

Dedicated to ___________________________ Date ________

Song Name	Artist	Year	Notes

URL ___________________________

Notes ___________________________

Playlist Title

Dedicated to _______________________   Date _______

Song Name	Artist	Year	Notes

URL _______________________

Notes _______________________

Playlist Title

Dedicated to ___________________________ Date _______

Song Name	Artist	Year	Notes

URL ____

Notes ____

Playlist Title

Dedicated to _________________________   Date _________

Song Name	Artist	Year	Notes

URL ____

Notes ____

Playlist Title

Dedicated to   Date

Song Name	Artist	Year	Notes

URL

Notes

Playlist Title

Dedicated to ___________________   Date ___________

Song Name	Artist	Year	Notes

URL ___________________________________

Notes ___________________________________

Playlist Title

Dedicated to   Date

Song Name	Artist	Year	Notes

URL

Notes

Playlist Title

Dedicated to ___________________________   Date ___________

Song Name	Artist	Year	Notes

URL ___________________________

Notes ___________________________

Playlist Title

Dedicated to   Date

Song Name	Artist	Year	Notes

URL

Notes

Playlist Title

Dedicated to ___________________________ Date ________

Song Name	Artist	Year	Notes

URL ___________________________

Notes ___________________________

Playlist Title

Dedicated to   Date

Song Name	Artist	Year	Notes

URL

Notes

Playlist Title

Dedicated to ___________________________ Date __________

Song Name	Artist	Year	Notes

URL _______________________________________

Notes _______________________________________

Playlist Title

Dedicated to   Date

Song Name	Artist	Year	Notes

URL

Notes

Playlist Title

Dedicated to ___________________________   Date ___________

Song Name	Artist	Year	Notes

URL ___________________________

Notes ___________________________

Playlist Title

Dedicated to ________________________ Date ________

Song Name	Artist	Year	Notes

URL ________________________

Notes ________________________

Playlist Title

Dedicated to   Date

Song Name	Artist	Year	Notes

URL

Notes

Playlist Title

Dedicated to ______________________________   Date __________

Song Name	Artist	Year	Notes

URL ______________________________

Notes ______________________________

Playlist Title

Dedicated to   Date

Song Name	Artist	Year	Notes

URL

Notes

Playlist Title

Dedicated to   Date

Song Name	Artist	Year	Notes

URL

Notes

Playlist Title

Dedicated to   Date

Song Name	Artist	Year	Notes

URL

Notes

Playlist Title

Dedicated to ___________________________ Date _________

Song Name	Artist	Year	Notes

URL _______________________________

Notes _______________________________

Playlist Title

Dedicated to

Date

Song Name	Artist	Year	Notes

URL

Notes

Playlist Title

Dedicated to ____________________________ Date ______

Song Name	Artist	Year	Notes

URL ____________________________

Notes

Playlist Title

Dedicated to   Date

Song Name	Artist	Year	Notes

URL

Notes

Playlist Title

Dedicated to _______________________ Date _______

Song Name	Artist	Year	Notes

URL _______________________________________

Notes _______________________________________

Playlist Title

Dedicated to ___________________________   Date ________

Song Name	Artist	Year	Notes

URL ___________________________

Notes ___________________________

Playlist Title

Dedicated to ______________________ Date ________

Song Name	Artist	Year	Notes

URL ______________________

Notes ______________________

Playlist Title

Dedicated to _______________________ Date ___________

Song Name	Artist	Year	Notes

URL _______________________

Notes _______________________

Playlist Title

Dedicated to   Date

Song Name	Artist	Year	Notes

URL

Notes

Playlist Title ___________________________

Dedicated to ___________________________ Date _________

Song Name	Artist	Year	Notes

URL ___________________________

Notes ___________________________

Playlist Title

Dedicated to _______________________ Date _______

Song Name	Artist	Year	Notes

URL _______________________________________

Notes _______________________________________

Playlist Title __________________________

Dedicated to ________________________ Date _______

Song Name	Artist	Year	Notes

URL __________________________

Notes __________________________

Playlist Title

Dedicated to _______________________ Date _______

Song Name	Artist	Year	Notes

URL ____

Notes ____

Playlist Title

Dedicated to   Date

Song Name	Artist	Year	Notes

URL

Notes

Playlist Title

Dedicated to ______________________________ Date ______________

Song Name	Artist	Year	Notes

URL ____

Notes ____

Playlist Title

Dedicated to   Date

Song Name	Artist	Year	Notes

URL

Notes

Playlist Title _______________________________

Dedicated to _____________________________ Date _________

Song Name	Artist	Year	Notes

URL ____

Notes ____

Playlist Title

Dedicated to

Date

Song Name	Artist	Year	Notes

URL

Notes

Playlist Title

Dedicated to   Date

Song Name	Artist	Year	Notes

URL

Notes

Playlist Title

Dedicated to   Date

Song Name	Artist	Year	Notes

URL

Notes

Playlist Title ____________________

Dedicated to ________________________ Date ________

Song Name	Artist	Year	Notes

URL ____________________

Notes ____________________

Playlist Title

Dedicated to ___________________________ Date _________

Song Name	Artist	Year	Notes

URL _______________________________________

Notes _____________________________________

Playlist Title

Dedicated to   Date

Song Name	Artist	Year	Notes

URL

Notes